Poet Robot

~

an introduction to
E.J. Wong

To Lee,
much love

−E

*Books by
E.I. Wong*

~

*The Captain's Society for Happy Cannibals
The Lunatic
The Book of Dave*

Poet Robot

~

E.I. Wong

PATCHY GIRL PUBLISHING
San Francisco, California

Poet Robot copyright © 2016 by Eric Wong. All rights reserved. Printed in the United States of Goddamn America. No parts of this book may be used or reproduced in any manner whatsoever without written permission except in the case of reprints in the context of reviews[*].

LCCN: 2016900391
ISBN: 978-0997135503

---

[*] With the exception of the word "goddamn," this paragraph was copied without permission from some random e-book on Amazon in an attempt to make the book appear more legit. Somehow saying "legit" in the copyright page makes everything seem less so. Also, this is suspiciously early in a book for footnotes. Sure hope this isn't a recurring thing...

Contents

~

"A Narcissist Writes Letters, To Himself"
... page 1

The Second Person
... page 43

Most of *Tin Lion*
or, the badge of heartless cowards
... page 83

to Patches

Poet Robot

an introduction to
E.J. Wong

"My pussy tastes like Pepsi Cola."
–Lana Del Rey, artist*

---

* Net worth, $8 million USD

E.I. Wong

"A Narcissist Writes Letters, To Himself"

Poet Robot

E.I. Wong

Woodsman

My grandfather was a man so brave
he once fought a bear with a chainsaw.

He lost.
Mostly because grandpa's ninety
& the bear had a chainsaw.

Poet Robot

Blackbeard, Seeking Insurance, Uncovers the Pirate Paradox

"So you have enough woodworking mastery
to construct & maintain ships worthy of transatlantic travel,
but when it comes to an effective prosthesis
you're going to settle with the 'peg approach?'

Oh, the ship is stolen...
Well that makes sense.

Wait, you have the thievery skills
to commandeer a vessel
with a crew of armed government employees
but you can't shoplift the lower half of a mannequin?

I don't mean to hark on the leg thing, but frankly

nothing about a self-employed alcoholic

gallivanting around a slippery, rocking ship deck on an unvarnished table leg

screams "insurable," Mr. Beard.
Did you have any questions?

...

I don't know about pillaging
but we do cover rape counseling
with a proper referral, of course.

No. No. No... We counsel the other side, Mr. Beard...
Yes, the victims."

E.I. Wong

CAROLE'S DEAD

A firefly's light

lights every single direction

except the direction the firefly is facing

& presumably traveling

which must be frustrating for the firefly

& might explain why you always see them

hovering aimlessly in circles

"No, Bob. You fly backwards by me

Keith spins in a circle

& I try to figure out where the frick Carole went.

She went flying off into the woods

once that bird started chasing her.

Carole's great at escaping, sure

but I don't know

as a species

we're pretty easy to follow around

at night."

A Shrill Shriek Follows Me[*]

My house is haunted
by a demonic talking skull
but nobody believes me
because it's wrapped in human flesh
& technically we're dating.

---

[*]This piece was written with the explicit permission of my real-life girlfriend who asked I clearly stat that I do not actually think she is an evil talking skull and that I love her very, very much. - e.i.

E.I. Wong

SERIOUSLY, DON'T BE AFRAID[*]

The Bible says in the End Times
fire will rain from the sky
but I'm not worried
I'm sure whatever's gonna try
to rain fire down from the sky
will be shot down
by the hellfire missile
of a predator drone.

---

[*] Always remember that the worst thing evil can ever do to you is kill you, and effectively liberate you from its presence. Anything short of that can be remedied with time and/or love. If for some reason you are being held captive by some evil person and they are keeping you alive, but won't allow you to have any contact with anything remotely loving/lovable, then this probably doesn't apply to you, but congratulations on finding and flipping through this book? I appreciate and love you for it. Sorry this one isn't for you. Next time.

Yep, just a daytime prom.

For my next car
I want something practical
like a limousine.

That way
when I'm at a light
the screams of young people
won't seem so out of place.*

---

* See? Super relatable to your predicament. You know, because you've been kidnapped? I'm really glad you're reading this book.

E. I. Wong

One clock, twice daily, every twelve hours

My doctor once said of depression,

*"There is no wound greater
than the one unseen;
which festers within
cutting without bleeding
weighing you down
robbing the appetite*

*& the less apparent our reasons for
suffering
the smaller and colder this insidious cage
becomes
its vicious whisper
insatiably demanding an unknown,
eating instead the heart & very will
to prosper
from your insides out."*

*He died of literally, the biggest tapeworm
you've ever seen,
which might account for some of that stuff,
but at the time it seemed really deep and
whatever...*

The reincarnation of good men[*]

A centipede with a foot fetish
has a genetic predisposition
for being really, really happy.

---

[*] "And if you're really good you get to stay dead!" - Life, aware that it is a prick.

EMPATHY

When someone is rude or lashes out at you
remember that it's almost never truly about you.
It is about the circumstances, trials and challenges
that particular individual inherited
through the conditioned fear responses of their parents
and culture.

But that's a little wordy
so alternatively
just imagine the human dildos of this world

as snowmen
who through no real fault of their own,
happen to hate the smell of carrots.*

---

* "Yeah, why don't you just go ahead and go fuck yourself..." - Life, to that snowman.

iHaiku

1 pm. porn break

after eating Hot Cheetos

worst idea ever.

E.I. Wong

You shouldn't need three[*]

If I could have any wish

I would wish to witness the moon landing

as the first two men took to the lunar surface.

& if I could have a second wish

I would wish that they would then hunt each other

for my amusement and hand in marriage.

---

[*] If you think you need more than two wishes to be truly happy, then maybe consider using that first wish to fill the hole in your heart you are currently attempting to drown with (I'm assuming) money, material possessions, or a much larger penis. You'll probably only need the one wish after that. It'll probably be for the larger penis.

Blog post from May 5th, 2015

Hello everyone.

After a confusing chain of emails
between the state government and myself
I learned that I was officially nominated
to become the Poet Laureate of California.

At first I thought I was being trolled
but have since learned that they were real government people
trying to fill an actual government position.

So I am officially launching my campaign
for the position of Poet Laureate
even though the job is not decided by any vote.
There's no democracy.
The governor just picks a guy (or girl).

"Then Eric, why launch a campaign?"

Because the governor has an email address.

You can contact him here:

https://govnews.ca.gov/gov39mail/mail.php

& you can tell him whatever you want.

"Well Eric, of course I support you, but what should I say to him?"

Gee, I dunno...
Off the top of my head?
Like some sort of fill-in-the blank,
copy-paste document?
Maybe something along the lines of,

E.I. Wong

**
Dear Governor Brown,

I, (your name here), resident of (city within the state of California) encourage you to select Eric "E.I." Wong to the position of Poet Laureate. Mr. Wong's work is (positive adjective), (even more positive adjective) and obviously the work of a handsome individual. One might even say his poetry is critical to the cannon of American literature, and even the English language. My words, not his. Mr. Wong himself is an upstanding citizen, with a caliber of likability equivalent to (beloved costumed vigilante), but unlike (beloved costumed vigilante) you can see his face, and guess what? Mr. Wong is handsome. Especially around the (body part) parts.

Mr. Wong in no way promised sexual favors in exchange for support of his fake campaign. Even though I love (your favorite sexual favor) and I would have happily exchanged the time it took to personally write this letter for said sexual favor, Mr. Wong is a man of such high integrity that despite multiple requests to (sexual favor) each other's (aforementioned body part), he very politely declined.

He really is a great guy, independent of being exceedingly attractive.

Sincerely,

(your name here)

Life lessons*

Here's how you end global warming through charitable efforts:

> 1. Host a bike marathon charity fundraiser for a green initiative that ends with the cyclists leaping off a ramp through a blazing ring of fire.
> 2. Replace pre-victory Gatorade Dixie cups with red cups of gasoline.
> 3. As the bikers cross the finish line, the spandex outfits with fake sponsors will catch fire, and melt into the cyclists' skin, grafting them to the bike permanently so they can forever clog up the road and make it impossible for cars to participate in the human miracle of the combustion engine.

---

* "Hahahahahahahahahahahahahahaha you think I'm here to teach you something. Idiot. I'm trying to replace you with something better!!" - Life, telling the truth.

E.I. Wong

                        So do you see how
                            in the end,
                  setting fire to fossil fuels
          in the immediate proximity of eco-activists
wearing sports equipment made from an oil bi-product
turns out to be the answer to climate change after all?

                    That's how that saying
              "hair of the dog that bit you" works.
                         Cool, huh?

Okay, son,

Daddy's gonna get another beer.

Get dressed, and I'll drive you to school.

Poet Robot

Relatable meme generator— Mark I

That awkward moment when

you and your ninja buddies

throw a surprise birthday party

for your other ninja pal

& you totally get him with the surprise

but then later everyone is standing around eating cake thinking,

"Haha, we could have murdered Dave."*

---

* Nothing like a reminder about how your closest friends and family are capable of colluding against you and ambushing you in your own home. Those party favors could very easily be swapped with blow-darts. You wouldn't have to change much else. Everyone still yells "surprise!"

E.I. Wong

THE DIRE CONSEQUENCES OF MISPLACED COMMAS

To-Do List:

Throw baby , shower

Poet Robot

PERKS OF THE INDUSTRY

IN AMSTERDAM
IF YOU DIE WITH NO NEXT OF KIN
AND NO ONE ATTENDS YOUR FUNERAL
A POET IS HIRED
TO WRITE AND RECITE A PIECE FOR THE SERVICE.

IT DOESN'T PAY A WHOLE LOT
BUT AT LEAST I CAN FINALLY START WRITING OFF
THOSE VATS OF HOMEMADE* "HOBO POISON"
AS TAX-DEDUCTIBLE BUSINESS EXPENSES.

---

* They never see it coming. You know, cause they don't have homes? #toomeanforTwitter

E.I. Wong

Our Perpetual Screaming Machine

Being an evil genius needn't be expensive.

Consider the simplicity and economic efficiency

of filling a merry-go-round with Alzheimer's patients

& donning one, very scary mask.

Poet Robot

The Hovercraft of Armament

Yesterday, I found myself

wanting to fly a kite

or at the very least

hitting a pelican with a harpoon

and then running around.

E.I. Wong

More Fun With String

Harpoons work wonders on land, too.
They needn't be constricted to the sea.

A shotgun wedding is one thing,

but with a harpoon wedding,

you can be sure

he ain't goin' *nowhere.*

Inner Peace

A good strategy for dealing with your enemies and cultivating inner peace is to forgive and forget.

Commonly, I call upon my enemies and forgive them of their crimes against me.
We gather, get merrily drunk,
I forget that I forgave them,
& then I shoot them in the leg.

Forgiveness really brings their defenses down. Shooting them in the leg brings down everything else.

E.I. Wong

This glass at half capacity

Under certain perspectives

everyday life looks tragic and dull

like watching a mime with no arms.

Yet with a bit of healthy detachment

and noticing little things

perhaps a powerful breeze

it can be beautiful, rich and quite often hilarious,

like watching a mime with no arms.

The Old Days

Before the internet

my brother and I

would sometimes kill the sunset hours

by tossing around the old pig skin.

Other times

we'd sneak out to the barn after dark

put on the old pig skin

& scare the living bejeezus

out of the orphan piglets.

She raised no quitters

Growing up, Mom always told us

to see everything through to the end

& to never be a hypocrite.

She lived and died by those words;

slumped over a

seven thousand piece puzzle

depicting a pile of puzzle pieces,

competitively eating a nine pound bag

of individually wrapped M&M's

& higher than the risen Jesus on LSD.

Plan for if this whole "Poet Laureate/Comedian" thing doesn't pan out

Phase 1

1. Open a chain of pirate-themed family restaurants.

2. Create novelty napkins featuring a treasure map for pirate themed family restaurant.

3. Bury treasure in accordance with said novelty napkin map.

4. Wait for someone to come looking for the treasure.

5. Abduct them.

6. Repeat steps 4 & 5 until local folklore or media frenzy is created.

7. Change treasure map napkin in a slight way, that only conspiracy theory weirdos would notice. (Or, create a new napkin designed in such a way that if you align it with the original napkin and then do a MAD magazine style fold it makes a whole new map)

8. Bury treasure in accordance with new novelty napkin map along with a note reading, "the victims are in the chicken." -Lee Harvey Oswald

9. With the media circus successfully distracted, convert all abductees from steps 4 & 5 into blood-thirsty pirates.

10. Along with blood-thirsty pirate crew,

commandeer several "Ride the Ducks" tourism crafts.

11. Temporarily satiate pirate crew's thirst for blood with tour guide body fluids.

12. Using the fleet of stolen duck trucks, storm the Governor's mansion.

13. Demand the Poet Laureate laurel wreath. Note how thirsty your pirate crew appears, then wink at the Governor (note: If wearing an eye patch, make sure you lift it up when you wink so the Governor knows you're not just blinking weirdly).

14. Lock eyes with the Governor's daughter.

15. Glisten.

16. Fall in love with the Governor's daughter.

17. Crown secured, contact your business card guy. See if he can add "pirate king" to recent order of "Eric Wong – Poet Laureate/Comedian" business cards.

18. Publicly declare self "Poet Laureate/Pirate King/Comedian." Show any naysayers some very official looking business cards.

19. While searching for stowaways, find Governor's daughter in a barrel of duck whistles.

20. Make her your pirate queen.

21. After a long, swashbuckling career and tiring of a life at sea, fake death via self-incited mutiny.

22. Escape with the pirate queen, using a life raft made from the same barrel of duck whistles you found her in.

23. During the long journey back to shore, realize that the raft cannot maintain both of your weight, and

allow pirate queen to wade in the water, sacrificing herself for your survival.

24. Years later, recover the nude painting she did of you from a sunken duck boat.

25. Recount your tales to archaeologists in painstaking, irrelevant detail that even archaeologists can't really be bothered with.

26. For no reason at all, cast priceless diamond into the sea[*].

---

[*]Author's note: Maybe "Write better poetry" should be a step... nah

E.I. Wong

Crimes Exposed

Recently I choreographed a children's flash-dance
& was immediately taken to prison.

Tarzan is offended

When a scientist says, "Chimps are our closest living relatives," that's really only true of orphans.

Run-ins with this ridiculous PC culture

Sure, I kid around a lot

but people actually think I was abused as a kid,

when in reality, they're just being overly sensitive.

Did Dad spank me from time to time?

Sure, but for the most part

throughout 99% of my childhood

the sex was really gentle.

Fables

While fishing on the river
I saw a beaver floating on a wooden plank.
It seemed stranded so I called to it,
"Are you okay?"

The beaver looked at me,
paddled over, shot me with a pistol
& said, "WELCOME TO THE GHETTO, M***** F******."

---

*   Author's note: I spent over three hours trying to decide on what expletive to use at the end of this post. At various points it ended with "moron," "jackass" and "honkey-ass bitch" the last of which was not chosen because I felt as though "honkey-ass bitch" would

*This page is dedicated to the rest of that really long foot-note. If you can't read text that small, it's basically about how my online audience didn't really care for the piece about the beaver. Look, I get it. I can't be "on" all the time, and given enough time I'm bound to misfire once in a while. The important thing is to not bring unnecessary amounts of attention to your blunders and just power through the bad times. People will forget the mistakes you make and forgive you once you rally with the good. The worst thing you can do is make a huge deal about messing up, and then try to over-explain the error with so much more explanation than is needed. It's pretentious.

---

suggest that the beaver was black, and thereby wrongly associate black culture with the ghetto. My girlfriend thought I was being stupid and overly-sensitive. I get that it is technically funnier if a beaver were to call me a "honkey-ass bitch" because I'm Chinese, but I felt that the joke was funny enough without the racial element. Upon publication, I received several messages from readers informing me that they did not find the piece funny at all. I have included it here, unaltered, because I don't give a shit what you think.

See Also: Predator Vs. Crocodile

Certain species of snake
see on the infrared spectrum
detecting differences in heat
between environment and prey.

But snakes are cold-blooded,
so they probably freak each other out all the time
& culturally, have a lot of really stupid "snake ghost" stories.

Raw Data

A study reported
that hired assassins
had some of the lowest divorce rates
which I found surprising
considering they're... oh

Biomimetics

Humanity's greatest innovations
start by studying the wild.
Our first understanding of medicine
came from watching the changes in eating habits
of sick or injured birds.

This continues today,
like how fish influence automobile aerodynamics,
or how the idea for Velcro came from burs on a dog
or the way bees taught the beauty industry
how to build an empire using, almost exclusively, bulimia.

E. I. Wong

UNDEAD ON THE INSIDE

I think if I came across a vegan zombie
a part of me would consider self sacrifice
just to sabotage the principles of the undead.

Who am I kidding?
Of course I would still
bludgeon their brains with a stick
just like the rest.

even if it's also a zombie.

Letter, Originally sent June 15th, 2015[*]

Dear Governor Brown,

Over the past few weeks, you may have received a number of suspiciously similar emails from "Californians" voicing their support for my nomination to the position of Poet Laureate. Of said emails, which by my estimate may have been about a dozen, at least one may or may not have invented sexual acts based on your wife, the first lady Anne Gust Brown, who I am assured is a very lovely and respectable woman.

I was not made privy to the details, so one can only speculate as to what those acts entailed. While we may surmise that Lady Brown's tenure as CEO of the GAP would encourage imagery that might or might not conflate the "GAP" with an orifice of the human anatomy, it would be shameful to do so and on behalf of your digital "constituents" I apologize. I'm sure the Lady Brown is a kind and modest woman. In fact, did you know you can rearrange the letters in Anne Gust Brown to "non-breast gun," which is Latin for, "not of the kind, or class: breast

---

[*] As of 12/04/2015 – It seems our dear friend Juan Felipe Herrera has taken to hoarding Poet Laureate positions. Not only has he become the U.S. Poet Laureate, but it appears as though the state of California will be giving Mr. Herrera a second term. Sure, it's a little greedy, but Juan earned it. Still, there is always next election cycle. If all this "emailing the Governor" business seems fun to you, feel free to continue to email the state of California continued requests to anoint me as the next Poet Laureate. I'm sure they won't mind. - e.i.

gun?" As if to think our illustrious governor would go and marry a pistol fit to fire nipples, or one of those Austin Powers sex robots... Although if he did, good for him. That's a very rare marriage equality/second amendment twofer.

Anyhoodle, hope this clears things up and that there are no hard feelings.

Best of luck with the drought,
Eric.

Poet Robot

Remember that really long footnote from before*?

Did you even read it?

I mean, I wouldn't be mad if you didn't.

The whole point of the footnote

is that you can go back and read it later if you want

and you technically don't have to read it at all.

But I did put a lot of work into it

and it does offer some cool insights into the writing process**

if that sort of thing interests you.

Just saying.

There's jokes in the copyright page too.

Get your money's worth.

If you're reading this in the library,

get a job.

Okay, now here's the big one...

---

* "Really being a dick about this one, aren't you?" -inner dialog, which I ignored.

** If patting yourself on the back for not being racist is part of the "writing process," then sure.

E.I. Wong

The Second Person
An experiment in comic poetry

Poet Robot

E.I. Wong

"Wait, why would you put a quote in the beginning of this? That's stupid." -my girlfriend, when asked what quote might set an appropriate tone for this piece.

Poet Robot

E.I. Wong

Episode 1: Hello, apprentice

Good assassins leave no trace of themselves.
They sneak in and out with no notice
& the loudest thing you'll hear is the sound of blood
dripping.

A great assassin leaves no blood.
There is no murder weapon
because a great assassin needs no mechanical advantage.
Think of it like how serious drivers
always drive stick.
With great assassins, the police have a hard time deciding
whether or not foul play was involved.
Maybe they did just choke on a chicken bone.
Maybe they did fall asleep smoking.
A great assassin's weapon of choice
is always Occam's razor.

The master assassin never walks in the room.
They never see their target in person.
The closest they get is an encrypted file on a computer
registered to someone else, and the names of the victims
are all changed.

How do we decode them?
Mostly guesswork.
But master assassins are mostly right when it comes to
these things.
That's what makes us masters.

With the master assassin, the police are never called.

Poet Robot

People are forgotten, like so many worn graves.
They understand that man is like a donkey
& that every donkey chases a carrot.
The master holds the carrot over a cliff
& the donkey undoes itself.

But you, my dear, are no master assassin.
That is a long ways off.

Come here.
Put these gloves on.
They're leather.
No lint.
Remember that.

This is a wrench.
You hit people with it.
It was paid for with cash
but still, think of it as a one-time use thing.
Everything is a one time use thing.

You want a knife?
Oh my silly, stupid apprentice.
Stupid, stupid apprentice.
What do you want to be, a walking talking poster for idiot prison bitches?
Why not just write "I killed a man"
on your chest using your victim's semen
& then going to a black light party?

Knives are for threatening people,
scaring people, or throwing a big display.
Knives are for thugs, musclemen and intimidators.
You cut things off with knives to make people remember

what loss is like.

You don't get to threaten someone with a wrench.
The only move is "beat to death."
You can technically warn them
of the impeding beating to death,
but that's not really threatening...

I don't want you over-thinking anything, apprentice.
For now just focus on calibrating your muscle memory
into knowing how much force it takes
to cave in a man's skull.

A mask?
You want a mask?
Why not make a mask out of your victim's semen,
call up the police yourself and say, "Hi, I just murdered a
man. You might want to go looking for some suspicious
sperm-smeared asshole with a wrench. I'll be sitting here by
myself handcuffing my feet to my dick."

Come on, apprentice.

No, you're going as yourself.
Cameron, the graduate student with dwarfism
who studies poetry.
That is the perfect mask.

Poetry.
Why didn't I think of that?
Honestly, there was a brief moment where I thought you
might already be a master assassin
because who in their right mind
would ever spend eight years of higher education

Poet Robot

learning about something so pointless as poetry?

It's the perfect cover.
"Oh look at me, I'm sensitive and I don't understand how
money works, boo hoo!"
Are you minoring in butter churning?
Maybe double majoring in porn film history,
back when all the ladies still had bushes?

You know, things that are pointless in America?

Hey, apprentice.
What's rhymes with "academic failure?"
"Poetry Major" sort of fits.
That's an off-rhyme.
See? Poetry is easy,
and I didn't even go to the first four years
of poetry undergrad.

Just joshing, apprentice.
I'm sure you'll be published.
Get that $1000 advance.
Collect on those mad poetry royalties.

But in the mean time,
take this.
It's a Bluetooth, a burner phone, a thermos,
& a pendant with a little camera in it.
I got it at a toy store by the wharf.

You'd be surprised how cheap and easy it is to acquire the
materials you need to create a fully functional spy network.

I think I've spent... Eighty dollars?

E. I. Wong

Plus tax.
What a time to be alive.
Or at least an assassin.

I know that's almost a tenth of your big future poetry
dollars, but keep in mind
I'm giving you 90k to do this
& that's just a small cut of what I'm getting.

Don't open the thermos.
Trust me.
It's crucial to the mission,
but don't open it until I tell you.

I'm serious, apprentice.
I'm watching everything through your pendant.
Your nipple has my eye in it right now.
Think of your nipples as my eyes.

Okay, you good to go?
I'll talk you through this.

The target is in the Main Library
in the San Francisco Civic Center.
It's perfect.
Lots of homeless crazies to blame it on,
& no security cameras
Because the government can't invade peoples privacy like
that.
Not here.

Not in America.

I know, right?

Poet Robot

What a bunch of idiots.

**

Alright, you're in.
Go sign up for a library card.
Use your real name.

Just do it, apprentice.
Trust me.
You have to think
the way the police think
you won't think.

Got it?

It doesn't matter.
Trust me, apprentice.
If you do one stupid thing,
they'll catch you.
If you do a bunch of stupid things,
they'll never suspect a thing.
Because what professional assassin
would leave their real name and address
at the crime scene
moments before carrying out a brutal murder?

By the way, apprentice,
I expect this murder to be brutal.
Like, he should be unrecognizable when you're done.
You should be aiming to cave his face in
just to make identification more difficult.
Also, that's why you should remember to take his wallet.
Make it look like a robbery.

Alright, now make your way up to the fifth floor.
Your target is looking at microfilm.
Use the stairs.
I don't want you getting into any charming conversations
with strangers.
If anyone asks, tell them you're looking for books about
sexuality in people with dwarfism.
Or poetry by dwarves. That sounds better.
Yeah, let's go with poetry by dwarves.
Hang on, lemme Google something really quick.

Good news, apprentice!
There are no famous dwarf poets.
You may have a shot after all.
But anyway, go murder that guy.

You see him?
He's the fat one at the microfilm reader
with the hoodie, fleece vest and sweatpants.
I know, right? It's like he doesn't even exist.
You'd think he was some loser.
That's what makes this one dangerous, apprentice.
Looking at him now, you'd never suspect that he'd have an
international bounty on his head.
You'd never expect him to have a gun in his fanny-pack.

No, you'd just think he was some fat, disgusting guy.
& he is.
It's beautiful really, how out in the open you can be with
heinous crimes
as long as no one wants to bang you.

But that is a lesson for a later day, apprentice.

Poet Robot

Actually, it's pretty short.

If you have to wear a disguise
make sure you make your face ugly.
People don't like looking at ugly people.
It makes you harder to identify.
Just remember not to make yourself too ugly,
or then you cross into "spectacle" territory.

Basically, anything like a goiter, or warts
or anything the social contract designated as, "rude to stare,"
will one hundred percent ensure that people will absolutely always stare.

It's like Goldilocks, but with facial deformities.

Alright, apprentice. You're up.
It's just you two on this for right now.
Chubs only does this work when he thinks no one is around.
Now, I can't technically tell you what he did
to deserve this, but let's just say for now
that it was a lot like that scandal
with the former Subway human mascot,
but with really, really old people.
Bad stuff.
It's fine.

Do you want to know?

You're not even curious?

I'm gonna tell you.

His name is Bernard.
He has a sexual fetish
where in order to climax
he has to be inside a person
as they die of natural causes.

Don't think about it, apprentice.
It only makes it worse.
Use that feeling to murder.
Go.
[I'm thinking about it now.]
Try to finish it in one swing.
I know you can do it.
Be quick, but more importantly be thorough.
That few seconds you use to take an extra face-scrambling swing
can buy you several hours of time while the police try to identify him.

Alright. Aim for the temple first,
then go to work on the face.

Good! See how easy that was?
Look how dead that guy is.
Okay, now do the face.
Nice.
Again.
Again.
I can still see face, apprentice.
Again.
Careful, you got blood on the camera.

Poet Robot

I can't see.
Okay, cool.
Again.
Again.
One last time for good measure.
Excellent work, apprentice.
Wow, alright maybe that's enough.
Calm down.
Smash quietly, apprentice.
You're in a library for Christ's sake.
People are trying to consume outdated information.
Take the wallet.
Good.

Okay, remember the thermos I gave you?
Go ahead and pour that bad boy on him.
Smell that?
That's moose pee.
Police will think this a clue of some sort
& waste a few hours figuring out
that this is moose pee,
that there are no meese in San Francisco
& that their suspect must come from a part of the world,
where moose pee is readily available for inter-state
transport.

Do you know what they won't be doing in that time?
Questioning a dwarf poet about murdering a fat dude.
Cause I'm a goddamn genius, apprentice.
Up top!
Or, well, up top for you.
Down low for me.

Get it?

Just yanking your chain, apprentice.
You can't high five me through your shirt.
But trust me, apprentice.
I high fived you in my mind.
I'm holding my hand up.
Are you?

Apprentice?

Are you holding your hand up?

Okay, I'm gonna assume you were and that we had a moment.
Get the hell out of there and meet me back at the Hockey Haven.

It's a bar, due west,
about five miles from you, near the ocean.

Leave the wrench and the thermos.
Over and out.

**

Oh hey, apprentice.
How're you feeling?
Good?
Empowered?
A little turned on?
Murdering a guy will do that to you.
They don't teach you that in school.

What're you drinking?

Poet Robot

We're celebrating.

A beer, eh?
Classic apprentice.
You're having two.
We're celebrating.
It's not everyday you get to trend on Twitter.

Oh, did you not see that?
#serialmoose?
They think you're a serial killer
And your calling card is drenching your victims in moose pee.

Yeah, who would have thought that moose pee
would have been so easily identifiable based on smell?
I guess those librarians are giant moose nerds
or maybe they're really into pee.
I imagine they deal with pee a lot.

Either way, the goose chase is on.
They'll never catch you.
Give me the equipment and then drink your drinks.

Oh wow, you drink fast.
Goddammit, why didn't I say "moose chase?!"
Whatever.
No, it's too late.
Don't... don't fake laugh.
It makes it worse.

Lemme tell you something about being an assassin, apprentice.

E.I. Wong

Over the years, we organized killers have been behind the
creation of a lot of fake serial murderers.

A lot of it is people doing things like the moose pee gag,
trying to throw off the scent.
But if you've been in this business for too long
you start to run out of ideas,
& maybe one or two things gets recycled.
Or maybe you and a buddy were throwing around ideas
& you both happened to like one
& you both happened to use that technique
without the other's knowledge.

Suddenly wham, bam everyone thinks
there's a moose pee collecting psycho on the loose.

But they'll never think a *midget* moose pee collecting psycho
is on the loose.
That would be ridiculous.
That's what makes you special, my tiny, tiny apprentice.

Now don't freak out,
But you still have some skull in your hair.
I got it.
It's okay.
Don't spaz.
I've eaten evidence before.
This won't be the last time either.

I like you, apprentice.
More than I thought I would.
To be honest, I thought you would be
like a one-time use wrench.
Some funny story I could tell the guys

Poet Robot

about how I murdered a guy with a midget.
A poet midget no less.

The thing about you,
& remember to always listen to a guy in a bar
who, three drinks in, claims to have figured you out,

But the thing about you is everyone probably expects a
dwarf poet to be sensitive
& no doubt you probably are,
but beyond that,
what I see in you is numbness,
a numbness that only a dwarf poet could have.

A numbness cultivated from sensitivity,
a numbness developed from a lifetime of shame and
ridicule,
constant mocking and misconceptions,
and in addition to the poetry,
you're also a dwarf.

And numbness makes for a great assassin.

Sensitive enough to be situationally aware.
Numb enough to do what needs doing.

You could go far in this world, Cameron.
Can I call you Cam?
That's a good assassin name.
Cam.
It fits too.
You're my little murder camera.

Dammit.

We're not trending anymore.
That was fast.
Oh great, people are fat shaming Vin Diesel* again.
I guess that is more important.
It was fun while it lasted.

Hang on..

 "looks like someone is getting pretty Fast and McFlurrious.
#chindiesel"

Another beer?

**

Wake up, apprentice.
Apprentice.
It's time to go.

You've been drugged.

Of course it was me. Who else?
I'm training you to be an assassin
& the first rule of assassins
is that after you hire someone to assassinate a guy,
you have to assassinate your assassin
so that it isn't traced back to you.

---

* In case you are reading this in the future: Vin Diesel is an American actor most known for his role in the *Fast and Furious* franchise, who frequently compares himself to great actors like Al Pachino. In sitcoms, if an actress got pregnant, directors employed various techniques to hide the baby bump (Big black peacoats, placing the actor behind a physical obstruction, or simply shooting from the bust up). Every single one of these techniques has been used on Vin Diesel. He is a forty-eight year old man (as of 2015), and everything he does is amazing.

Poet Robot

Don't worry, I just roofied you.
In real life you'd be poisoned dead.
You gotta look alive, apprentice.
Never trust anyone.
Except me.
I'm the only one you can trust.
I know I just drugged you
but I didn't kill you, did I?
Pretty trustworthy, no?
I could have done all sorts of stuff to your butt, just to prove a point, but did I?

How about a thank you?
Some gratitude would be nice.

Alright, I can tell you're feeling a little defensive.
I'm just perceptive like that.

You really can trust me, apprentice.
I want you to succeed at this.
I want you to succeed me, in fact.
I see something in you.

All the lessons you learn in this field
are hard lessons.
Put the Bluetooth back in.
It's time for lesson two.

While you were out, I tweeted the San Francisco police.
They're on their way here now, and you need to hide.
Trial by fire, apprentice.
This should be a pretty easy one for you though, right?
You can fit in things.

Oh look, they're here.
I'm gonna walk right out the front door,
smile at them and be on my merry way.
Don't copy me.
Only one of us can use that move.
It looks suspicious otherwise.

Later, Cam.
I'll see you on the other side.

\<zkt^\>

There is a window in the men's room.
You might want to try sneaking out that way.

Apprentice?
Why aren't you moving?
Don't just sit there, you need to go!
Why are you just staring at that beer bottle?

Don't be stupid, apprentice.
There are two cops
And one bottle.
What did I tell you?
Everything is one time use.

Also, DON'T ATTACK THE COPS IN BROAD DAYLIGHT.
ARE YOU INSANE?

Crap.
Did they hear that?
Look left, apprentice.
No, the other left.

Poet Robot

Why are they leaving?
They heard me, didn't they?

Okay, change of plan, apprentice.
Attack them with the beer bottle.
Go on.
Distract them.
Crack the bottle over one and then slash the Achilles
tendons of the other with the shards.

Apprentice, I'm not hearing the agonized screams
of public servants.

Ohmygodohmygodohmygod they're coming.
Quickly, apprentice! Tweet the police!
Draw them away.
Call 911 and say you're being raped by foster children.
They'll buy that.
Police hate foster kids...
Crank call the police, apprentice!

Wait, they're stopping.
Did you call?

Stay calm, apprentice.
Leave this to a master assassin.
Someone of your rank and stature
couldn't possibly get away with murdering two on-duty
police officers in broad daylight

But we're not talking about you.
Watch and learn, apprentice.
This is how a real assassin... Assassinates...

E.I. Wong

**

Apprentice, the assassin's most frequently used tool
Is the element of surprise
followed closely by stealth.
They are your right and left hands.
Did you see how stealthily I stole the police car,
& how surprised the cops were
when I ran them down with their own vehicle?

You should be taking notes, apprentice.
Don't actually take notes.
That's leaving evidence.

Speaking of which, hand me that can of gasoline.
It's time to burn some corpses.

As an assassin, you have some big boots to fill.
Literally.
Wear shoes that are too big for you.
The footprints will throw off anyone on your trail.
If they're looking for a guy with size elevens
they aren't going to stop you.
Oh my god, you would look adorable in size elevens,
apprentice.

Do we have time to switch shoes?
No. Damn.
Next time, apprentice.
Next time.

Proper body disposal is an important skill for any aspiring
assassin.

Poet Robot

Now, is burning some corpses in the middle of Golden Gate Park on a Tuesday afternoon ideal?

No. It isn't.

But an assassin is nothing if not adaptable.
Hopefully this will all be blamed on the homeless.
Over the years, I have blamed a lot of murders on the homeless.
I've put countless in prison, which is sort of a home,
so really I'm just doing my part. You gotta give back, you know?
I don't really donate to charity otherwise.

Anyway, once we finish here
it's back to the Hockey Haven.

Come on, don't look at me like that.
Have I taught you nothing?

Of course we have to go back.

What cop killers would return to the scene of the crime
a mere ninety minutes after running down two police officers?

They'd never expect us to do that.

If we get there and something happens
just let me do all the talking, apprentice.

If there's any trouble I'll give you the signal
& then you start murdering people.

E. I. Wong

Hm?

I don't know what the signal is yet.
I'll probably just blink, or move my hand in a funny way.

Trust me, apprentice.
An assassin is intuitive
& flows with the moment.
You'll know the signal when you see it.

**

Okay, so what we've learned
is that we should decide on a signal beforehand.

In retrospect, I should have told you
that I like to wave my arms around a lot I speak to law
enforcement.

I'm theatrical like that,
when I'm pulling one over on the cops.

Never you mind, apprentice.
A little bit of corpse burning never hurt anyone.
It really builds that assassin character.

You see now this is the second fire we've started in Golden
Gate Park.
The sun isn't down,
& I'll bet there's a story brewing somewhere
about a serial arsonist.

But will they connect this to the moose pee?
Doubtful.

Poet Robot

We don't even have anymore moose pee to leave.
& it's not like you started a corpse fire in the library.
You didn't start any corpse fires in the library, right?
Apprentice.
Look me in the eye and tell me
you didn't secretly loop footage on your nipple cam
so you could sneak away and set fire to the corpse in the library.

Okay, I believe you.

Anyway,
This is how you create pandemonium, apprentice.
I've made a lot of pandemonium in my days.
Chaos is an effective cover.
People rarely remember intricate face details
when they're running away from you and for their lives.
They're usually more concerned with themselves.

And the thing about the police
is that when shit gets crazy
they tend to slow down.

Sure, they're looking for us in the trees somewhere,
But they think we're mad dangerous
So they're gonna stick close and walk slow.

You know what that means, right?
Right.
We have to be recklessly fast
& split up.

You have your Bluetooth, apprentice?
Good.

E. I. Wong

See those lights?
That's the police.
Don't go that way
unless you plan to murder more city employees.

Wait, apprentice, did you want to just double back
And assassinate these guys?

We could.

You sure?

Apprentice...
Might be fun...

Fine.

Party pooper.

Alright, let's do this.
You walk north and head for the golf course,
I'll go west and lose them in the ocean.
Cops can't swim.
They hate the water.
To them, it might as well be a giant mass of foster children.

We'll meet later tonight
& I know you're going to think this is a bad idea
but I need you to trust me, apprentice.

I need you to trust me
& in four hours
You will meet me
at the Hockey Haven.

Poet Robot

**

See, apprentice? What did I tell you?
The Hockey Haven is the perfect place to meet.
No police.
Everyone is in the park.
And look, several internet news sources are saying
that a rogue cop may have been the culprit.

You know,
the old, cop couple kills another cop couple,
then the first cop couple start squabbling,
& the first cop from the first cop couple,
shoots the second cop from the first cop couple,
sets the car on fire,
shoots himself in the head,
& the body falls into the trunk and the trunk closes with
both bodies inside.

It's a tale as old as time.

The police have said the reports are untrue,
but don't you think that's exactly what they would say
to hide the embarrassing truth?

Now, apprentice, I didn't say they had to be credible news sources.
I mean, do I control some of those accounts?
A master assassin never reveals his secrets.

Okay, yeah it was me.
I've been tweeting the shit out of that story.

E.I. Wong

The #blacklivesmatter people are picking it up.
I don't know why.
All of those cops were bl... Oh.

I'm sure it'll just throw them off even more.
That's cool.

Oh my God.
Apprentice.
Something amazing has happened.

Vin Diesel has blocked me on Twitter.

**

Good morning, apprentice.
Did you sleep well?

Yes, I drugged you again.
To see if you had learned.
You didn't.

Here, have some water.
The roofies really dehydrate you.

Good!
You didn't drink the water.
I'm glad.
This water has all kinds of poison in it.
I was worried if you had fallen for that three times
I would have to go find another apprentice.

Do you know any other dwarf poets?

Poet Robot

Maybe ones who aren't so poison stupid?

Just joshing, apprentice.
You're great.
While you were sleeping
I made this Vine of the nipple cam.

Look at you go,
It's like his face never runs out of blood and face guts.
This is another important lesson in the assassin world.
You know how I said that assassins often are assassinated
for their knowledge of their own assassinations?

Documenting certain pieces of vital information
to use against whoever may want you dead
offers a limited amount of protection.

For instance, take this Vine.
I know I just drugged you and maybe tried to poison you a little
& that is plenty reason to want to kill me.

But now that I have evidence
linking you to a murder,
I can be assured
that you will try your very hardest
to stay the Satan's testicles off my shit list.

Blackmail and assassinry often cross paths.
You will learn the art of blackmail at a later time.

Today, we work on survival.
You may be wondering where exactly we are.

E. I. Wong

I'm not going to tell you.

We're still in California
& I promise that I won't be too far off,

but right now
I'm abandoning you in the woods.

As an assassin,
you will probably find yourself on the run from the law,
especially if you're a bad assassin,
& by the looks of things, apprentice,
I'd say you're not great.

But that's why you have me.

I kind of got tired of telling you to put in your Bluetooth,
so I super glued it into your ear.
Hope you don't mind.
Now I'm in your head forever, apprentice.

Forever.

Look at me, apprentice.
I don't want you peeking at where I'm sneaking off too,
so I've arranged a sort of training drill.

When you are in the wild
you may encounter animals.
In all my experience as a master assassin
what I have learned
is that the best option in almost all scenarios
is to attack the Nature as quickly as possible.
Swiftly.

Poet Robot

With no remorse.

If you don't eat them,
they will eat you.

And this brings us to these cages of raccoons.
As you can see, they have some pretty severe rabies.

Remember my words, sweet beautiful apprentice,
& Godspeed to you.

**

Oh my God, apprentice.
You know what?
I totally forgot that I used the same number of raccoons on
you that I use for the regular-sized assassins.
I did not scale that test at all.

In retrospect, that was way too many raccoons.
You just fought twice your body weight
in rabid raccoon.

Apprentice?
Can you hear me?
How are you doing?

Oh man, you're gonna need all kinds of rabies shots.
It's okay, apprentice.
In normal cases,
You have around seventy-two hours to get the shot,
so I'm sure you have at least a few hours.
That's plenty of time.

E.I. Wong

You sure gave them hell, though.
Those baby raccoons were terrified.

Did they scare you?
You can tell me.
This kind of feedback is really important.
Weren't they scary?
It was so hard giving the babies rabies
because the mom doesn't want to bite them naturally
but I did it for the effect
& I think it came through.

Did you hear that, apprentice?
It sounded like law enforcement.

Since I kind of gave you a handicap with the whole
too many raccoons thing, I'm gonna cut you a break and tell you now
that I didn't really abandon you in the woods.

You're in Golden Gate Park.
Those are the cops.
You should run.

**

How did I know?
Apprentice?
How did I know I would find you here?

They should rename this place
the Assassin Haven.
This beer is your mana potion, apprentice.
Thank yo...wait a minute.

Poet Robot

Apprentice, did you drug this drink?

I know that would be pretty justified
 what with the whole coon fiasco.

[That's not what I meant, madam.

Well, I do apologize.
No, I was explaining to my friend here
that he would be justified in drugging me with a roofie
because I made him fight a family of raccoons.
The animal.

No you're crazy!] Haha, we have fun, don't we, apprentice?

Apprentice, I swear to God,
If I drink this drink
& pass out due to anything other
than self-induced alcohol poisoning,
I will eat your brains in my eggs.

Oh.
You didn't.
Very good then.

Honestly, I'm a little upset you didn't try to poison me or anything.
You know just,
as an educator,
It would be nice to know that...

E.I. Wong

Well that something is sinking in, you know?

No, it's too late for that.
Now I'll know you're trying to poison me
& it's not the same.
It's fine, apprentice.

Let's finish up here & get you that rabies vaccine.

**

A true assassin
has only one joy in life.
The battle.

And to compress that elation
of murder
into a single instance
or draw it out in a shower lasting eons
casting death upon entire generations
& immortalizing your cruelty in history and legend,
is the art of assassinry.

And like in any art
there are hacks.

I refuse to train some hack assassin.

Apprentice, the only reason you should be around piano wire
is if you are playing the piano.

Piano wire is uncomfortable
& it totally ruins a perfectly good piano.

Poet Robot

Do you know what it takes to repair a piano?
You have to call a guy.
It's an appointment.
Small talk.

& you know every single goddamn piano man
has the same stupid jokes about fixing a single piano string.

Sure that's fine the first time,
but let's be real, of course someone was murdered.

Why else would one piano string break?
Did Kanye come over and play one of his songs live for you for nine hours?

Okay, maybe he would do something like that.

Hang on, I'm gonna see if that'll fit in a tweet.

Ah, no that is way too long.
Should I do a bunch of tweets?

No, I don't want to be that guy.

Apprentice, you never want to be a "guy."
It's hack.

You gotta do things like the moose pee.
Something so eye catching
it blinds them to what's really there.
You can't look past the moose pee.

If you don't change things up

they catch you.
& like anything else,
doing the same thing over and over gets boring.
You end up just going through the motions
of mindlessly slaughtering bad guys for money
instead of living and engaging with your craft.

Money's the real thing you gotta watch out for.
Money will make you lazy and desperate.
It will make you boring.

We do this because it's awesome.

Now, I know what you're thinking.
Why are we at a veterinary office instead of a hospital?

Well, apprentice, I don't know if you ever seen a mafia movie,
but those guys always use vets instead of doctors.
Doctors are obligated to call the police.
Vets are usually hippies, and therefore very easily coerced.
They love animals.
If you know how to pretend to torture a puppy,
you know how to get free medical care.

Don't worry apprentice,
if you don't know how to pretend to torture a puppy,
you can just for-realsies torture it.
It works just the same.

Apprentice.
Don't look at me like that.
I can read your mind apprentice.
My voice is literally in your head.

Poet Robot

This is not a hack thing to do.

This is honoring your lineage.
There is an important difference there.

This is a killer's tradition.
It's like our Christmas tree,
but you put a scalpel to little Donut's pug face here.

[Seriously ma'am, dog hostage situation aside,
this is the cutest pug in the world.]
I'm totally taking him with us.

[What? Nothing. Keep sewing]

Hey, apprentice.
It's like reverse Stockholm Syndrome.

But it's Dogholm Syndrome.
[Oh yes it is!]

Don't look at me like that, apprentice.
There is too much adorable going on right now.

And by the way,
you remember what I told you, right?
About eaving-le oh-ne evidence...eh?
In regards to the et-veh? Eh?

What I'm saying is,
you're looking pretty well patched up.
You got the rabies shot.
Everything is good.
Now it's just a matter of how we keep this vet here quiet.

E.I. Wong

You hear how she's begging and pleading?
They all do that.
All the time.
No matter what.
It doesn't change the fact that you have two options
deemed acceptable by the assassin's way.

You can either
bring her into the fold and earn her trust
through a series of sexual advances and putting her in
perilous situations
that condition her to rely on you
or you can get with the stabby-stabs.
No, don't stab.
Stabbing leaves evidence.
I mean, kill her if you want,
but don't make a mess, you know?

[She gets it, doesn't she Mr. Donut?]

Again, it's not hack.
It's tradition.

I'll let you decide what you want to do.
I'm gonna take my new best friend here outside
so I can hit on jogging women.

To be continued[*]

---

[*]for more adventures with Cam Hatchet, check out "Detective's Log," available at notesfromanarcissist.wordpress.com

Poet Robot

E.I. Wong

Selections from

OR, THE BADGE OF HEARTLESS COWARDS

Poet Robot

E.I. Wong

On having kids

I would love to have kids one day,
to take part in the great human tradition
of convincing children there are such magically
wonderful things like Santa Claus.

I remember my own father
who tried so hard to convince us kids Father
Christmas was real;
how he'd dress up as Santa every year
sneak through the house
just loud enough to wake us

come into our rooms
late at night
with his fake beard and bag
lay on top of us
and laugh.

Poet Robot

10 reasons your relationship isn't working

Your partner loves being fingered.

You have no hands.

20:20

Of course, in hindsight,
"laser tag" was way more marketable
than "children's murder simulator."

Poet Robot

Dumbo Goes Rambo on Literacy

I was in the library
and saw a book called
"Teaching Kids to Read for Dummies."

It was a one page document
that read, "Please don't."

E.I. Wong

This piece is titled, "Untitled."

Just once, I'd like a DVD to express the views and opinions of 20th Century Fox and its affiliates, because what are they *really* thinking?

Vegan Relativity

I want to stop animal cruelty
and be kinder to our fellow creatures,
but that's a lot of work,
so I'm just meaner to people instead.

E.I. Wong

however fleeting

I'd like to think,
when I walk face first into a spider web,
there's a brief moment
where the spider thinks it's his lucky day

Followed quickly
by that feeling that you've bitten off
way more than you can chew
but like times a thousand.

Last words

"… And I would like to be remembered
as a man who never discriminated
against anyone, even the severely
retarded," the axe murderer decreed.

In the moments before execution,
he told the victims' families
just how resilient and strong the deceased were,

later clarifying,
he meant how difficult it was
to dismember their flailing bodies.

E.I. Wong

The PR Campaign

Of Noah's many achievements
his greatest is by far
purifying humanity

through the holy equivalent of "insider trading"
& overseeing widespread systematic incest
for nine-hundred and fifty years.

But yeah, let's just focus on the boat thing…

Poet Robot

To Describe Blowjobs Artistically[*]

> "The master of ceremonies asked people to say what they thought the function of the novel might be in modern society, and one critic said, 'To provide touches of color in rooms with all-white walls.' Another one said, 'To describe blow-jobs artistically.'" -Kurt Vonnegut, Slaughterhouse Five.

Few individuals share the experience of enlightenment exactly as Oscar's. Drunk, in the back seat of a 20-something Honda Civic, being blown ever so graciously by God-knows-what-her-dad-named-her, Oscar peered into the left tilted rear-view mirror only to see Tiny Jesus smiling and waving from the driver's seat headrest. Thinking this was some strange, unknown hallucinatory side-effect of drinking tequila with raspberry vodka, Oscar tried to

---

[*] From "The Book of Dave"

refocus on the petite, curly haired red-head
slobbering all over his phallus of fluctuating
firmness.

Yet he found himself closing his eyes. He found
himself thinking about doing history homework
in between laundry cycles, his childhood go-to
for erection stifling. God-knows-what-her-dad-
named-her looked up and asked if everything
was okay: the mast was drooping. Oscar
reassured her that everything was wonderful.
Everything was dandy. Tiny Jesus definitely
wasn't playing a harmonica on the dashboard.

In just a moment Oscar will have his mind
divided from his body. He will be gone long
enough such that when he returns the only thing
he will see are the curly maroon pubic regions of
a faceless, nameless, inhabitant of the planet

who he will love and understand deeper than the man who named her. She will be completely unaware that the mind, formally attached to the body, attached to the member in her mouth, has been shown the shadow of the nature of existence. As Oscar's mind leaves for an indescribably present yet distant sense of time, the beast within this soulless man will occupy her with pulsating gyration of up, down and up, and she will sync up with him, her fishy lipstick going down, up and down.

Tiny Jesus moves from the dashboard towards Oscar in a four-dimensional trajectory. How best to describe this? At rest he is one, making a singular decision. In motion, he is many and all possibilities on a sliding scale of probability. Oscar can only perceive a kaleidoscopic view of a thousand Tiny Jesuses teleporting towards him,

until one appears atop the ginger girl's head
going down, up and down, her hot, gin scented
fumes of nose breath moistening Oscar's thigh.
Tiny Jesus's little feet deform her hair, but she
doesn't seem to notice. Tiny Jesus takes out his
harmonica again and blows a harsh sweep from
low to high, and as the top note stabilizes,
everything glows whiter, and whiter, and up,
down and up again.

And this is what Heaven is like: Tiny Jesus is
normal Jesus again, and you enter mid-stride
with your eyes on Jesus's open palm. He is
offering you a handful of sunflower seeds. You
walk along a river, on a soft dirt path, barefoot
and surrounded by miles of plush, twig-less
grass. As you know from Tiny Jesus in the car,
there is no talking here; just a knowing gleam of
eye contact. There is never any confusion, so

there is no need to say anything. No decisions have to be made because everything will be just fine. If you don't like sunflower seeds, you don't have to take them, but Jesus being Jesus, he will always offer. When Jesus eats sunflower seeds, he doesn't eat them one at a time. He doesn't even bother to de-shell them. He throws them into his mouth a handful at a time and chews the wad like gum. From time to time, between wads, he wades into the water and takes a long drink. He doesn't mind getting wet from the belly down. Sometimes there is a warm breeze and sometimes there isn't. Sometimes it is a cooling wind and sometimes not. No one really notices because either is just fine. People are the same as they were on Earth, and everyone is here.

You walk on with Jesus, in the ever pleasant day. He spits wads of sunflower shells into the grass, and always offers you a handful. All the while, you pass by pairs of true lovers, silently engaged with an art or craft in the warmth of each other's company. Once dead, everyone becomes a master of their art, and no one remembers why there were art critics to begin with, until they really think about it. They understand, smile, or laugh to themselves and forget all over again. A book is no better than a painting, nor worse, and a painting is no better or worse than any other painting. They are simply different. When pairs pass by other pairs, they look over each other's work and smile with warmth and knowing. There is no need to praise, because the artist knows the work is a masterpiece, so the subject just enjoys the art for what it is, and everything is just fine.

You walk by Hell every now and again, and

everyone in there is the same as they were on Earth. Looking from the outside in, Hell is a massive, light gray, concrete pyramid full of windows and balconies for people to smoke on, because you aren't allowed to smoke indoors, even in Hell.

There was never any torture, or fire. They just prefer to be indoors, despite the ceilings being a little low, and the lighting poor. That was the only difference. Low lighting and low ceilings. People in Hell, which isn't that bad of a place at all, would simply rather stay indoors on a perpetually sunny day, or a surprisingly warm evening. The inhabitants of Hell have the Internet, television, and bars. They will sometimes come out to an overhang, or a patio to smoke cigarettes, because even in Hell, you can't smoke indoors. You work the same job you had on Earth in Hell, and everyone makes as much as they need to. The people of Hell pay taxes, although the tax money doesn't really go anywhere. There is no governing body, because no one is worried about theft or murder, because everyone has all the material items they could want, but are silently uncomfortable with admitting that empty feeling associated with having too many luxuries.

Not too many people know how the monetary system in Hell works, but there are lots of television shows that talk about it, and everyone understands that it is meant to be confusing. There are lots of hand sanitizer stations and pay-phones that no one uses. They all have their own private space, and there is plenty of it, although the ceilings are a little low, and the lighting poor.

Poet Robot

In Hell, they provide you with just enough room to be lonely in, and a cavalcade of luxuries that don't really matter. You have the best hot tub so nice it gets just a little too hot, and the most powerful air conditioner so it's almost always a little too cold, and most people spend their days getting in and out of really nice hot tubs and re-watching their same favorite television programs. You have an endless supply of TV channels, but you probably only watch programs on about four or five of them. You have a computer with Internet to watch the shows you watch on TV, or read the ideas of other people watching TV on a computer.

People in Hell still spend a lot of time on cell phones, because they aren't comfortable with accepting the silent knowing that the folks in

Heaven have. They know the same things that the Heaven folk know. They just still need someone to validate them. People in Hell aren't unhappy at all. They just aren't sure if they're happy. They aren't sure of a lot of things, like if they know the same things that the folks in Heaven know. They do. It's just not enough.

There are still bar fights. There is still work drama. They still defecate in Hell because they still eat, and they eat well. But toilets still get clogged, and people still gripe as they either call a plumber or search for a plunger. They know they've died, and there is no real need to eat beyond pleasing the sensation of hunger. Besides, Jesus eats too. Jesus poops also. He likes to visit Hell sometimes with a smattering of Heaven folk who could be bothered, and they will go find a place to eat a slice of pizza, or a roll of sushi. No one is quite sure how it all started, but for whatever reason Jesus loves tuna salad mixed with macaroni and cheese, topped with capers, jalapeños and chunks of thickly sliced turkey bacon. No one is quite sure where he gets it either, but everyone is comfortable not knowing certain things.

Asking how often Jesus gets tuna salad mixed with mac and cheese with capers, peppers and bacon is a silly question for the dead because there is no time. There is day, which is always pleasant, and night, which is always surprisingly warm, but no one in Heaven pays any attention to the change for being too deep in the enjoyment of the moment, and everyone in Hell is in a perpetual state of coming out of a movie theater and being shocked by the state of the day, so they are no help at all. What can be said about Jesus's visits to Hell is that when he walks around, everyone knows him, but they often call him by different names – again, it is mostly out of this strange need for Hellian validation despite knowing exactly who he is. They call him Buddha, Mohammad, Moses, Vishnu, Holiness, Steve and all sorts of names, and he responds to them all with a wide smile and a handful of sunflower seeds. People in Hell rarely eat sunflower seeds. They have no proper place to spit.

People in Heaven are allowed to stay in Hell, and people in Hell are allowed to go to Heaven, but you rarely stay in both places equally. Part of that unspoken understanding is knowing where you prefer to be, and everyone is just fine with it. No one tells people they don't belong anywhere, they just give knowing smiles signifying an acknowledgment of a stranger or a neighbor, and there is very little difference between the two. Sometimes you see a pale pudgy Hell girl going for a run along the river, and everyone from Heaven chuckles because they forgot what being in a rush was like. Sometimes you see a person from Heaven walking dazed around a mall in Hell, sipping a Slurpee and staring at mannequins and pondering what possible good a fine Italian suit would do on a beautiful day like this. It would only get ruined in the river, so they never go inside.

The most overlap you see between inhabitants of Heaven and Hell is the library. Everyone likes the library. People from Heaven love fiction from Hell. They love the adventure, the noir, the mystery and excitement of murder stories, but they love it in the library, knowing that it will all

go back on the shelf shortly. People from Hell
love the poetry from Heaven. It helps them
appreciate natural beauty in that slightly
removed medium they are so used to. It is a nice
break from watching nature shows on the latest
3D HD TV technology; they still don't have
leave the comforts of their home; they can still
drink premium coffee that is just a bit too
strong, and smoke cigarettes that are a smidgen
too heavy, knowing peacefully enough, that it
will all go back on a shelf.

You wonder the same thing everyone wonders
when they take their walk with Jesus eating
sunflower seeds. Did Jesus ever get blown? And
knowing the "did-Jesus-ever-get-blown" look like
his own reflection in the river, he smiles at you,
and you realize that knowing either way would
have been disappointing. For those of you who

have died, everything becomes clear at this point, but for folks like Oscar, he chuckles – the only real verbalization in Heaven – and you continue on, leaving a trail of sunflower shell wads behind.

E.I. Wong

It's A Good Thing I Never Became a Billionaire

My teacher asked me what I wanted to be
when I grew up.
I said I didn't know.
My teacher asked what I would do
with a billion dollars
& had all the time in the world.

I said I would build airports that smelled like
churches
and churches that smelled like airports,
sit in a Cinnabon all day,
(because The Church of Eric has Cinnabons at
every location)
and watch people go by,
smelling the air,
confused.

Poet Robot

My teacher put on Ferris Beuller's Day Off,
put her head down on her desk
& later left the room when Ben Stein appeared
which is an appropriate thing to watch
when someone loses faith in humanity.

I never saw my teacher again,
which wouldn't have been an issue
had I not been home-schooled.

E.I. Wong

The End.

01010101 00100000
01101110 01100101
01110010 01100100

shift + (,#)

Poet Robot

Eric "E.I." Wong lives in San Francisco with his cat, George. He attended the University of Oregon for poetry where he was not well received. Despite completing the requirements for a Creative Writing minor, the department did not give it to him. He is not bitter about this at all. He currently works at the San Francisco Public Library's[*] Access Services department, helping blind, deaf and physically handicapped patrons for very little money because he is a really good guy.

& you know what? He's not bad looking either.

---

[*] The views and opinions expressed in this book of poetry *explicitly represent* the views and opinions of the city and county of San Francisco and all of its affiliates. You might as well title this book "The views and opinions of the city and county of San Francisco and all of its affiliates." When reviewing this book, please make sure you mention that these are the literal views and opinions of every single godforsaken San Franciscan & anyone affiliated with said San Franciscan. I speak for them now.

Made in the USA
Charleston, SC
03 February 2016